BITE-SIZE
LINCOLN

Other Bite-Size Books

Bite-Size Twain, by John P. Holms and Karin Baji
Bite-Size Einstein, by John P. Holms and Jerry Mayer

BITE-SIZE
LINCOLN

Wit & Wisdom from
the Frontier President

COMPILED BY JOHN P. HOLMS AND KARIN BAJI

ST. MARTIN'S PRESS ❧ NEW YORK

THOMAS DUNNE BOOKS.
An imprint of St. Martin's Press.

Library of Congress Cataloging-in-Publication Data

Lincoln, Abraham, 1809–1865.
     Bite-size Lincoln : wit & wisdom from the
frontier president / compiled by John P. Holms
and Karin Baji.—1st ed.
        p.   cm.
"Thomas Dunne books."
ISBN 0-312-19240-1
1. Lincoln, Abraham, 1809–1865—
Quotations.   I. Holms, John P.   II. Baji, Karin.
III. Title.
E457.99.B35   1998
973.7'092—dc21   98-23894
                       CIP

First Edition: November 1998

10 9 8 7 6 5 4 3 2 1

Contents

Preface

Abraham Lincoln was a quotable man and, indeed, many men have quoted him saying memorable things as far back as his early years in Springfield, Illinois. In assembling this book, we have taken great care to distinguish words attributable to the man Lincoln, from others belonging solely to his myth and legend. Whether we succeeded or not, not even Abraham Lincoln could say. In his own lifetime, our sixteenth president had a hard time separating what he said from what was said about him. And, chances are, if it was a good joke or anecdote that helped to make his point, he would retell it happily.

Lincoln's own difficulty in claiming authorship is compounded today by our own modern expectations of originality. To quote a person today is to cite that person as author and originator of a phrase or idea. Yet originality was no more a concern of Lincoln in his speechmaking or storytelling than it was of his listeners. Rhetorical wisdom of the day urged that, when ears are ringing, they're apt to listen more closely. And Lincoln, like his contemporaries, chose words and sayings that would strike his listeners as familiar. When he admonished his audience that "A house divided against itself cannot stand," he was not only echoing but, assigning his case the full force and dignity of the Gospel According to St. Mark: "If a house be divided against itself, that house cannot stand."

Lincoln's "A House Divided" speech illustrates a second problem of citation, that of historical context. Although these words were spoken by senatorial nominee at an Illinois Republican state convention, and had to do with expanding, not abolishing slavery, posterity has mistaken the "house" of mention to be Congress and its division to be that of a warring North and South. In this instance, learning the context of a quote restores, rather than diminishes its oratorical effect; surely Lincoln's words reverberated all the more because they alluded to a greater threat looming over the nation.

In other instances, a century and a half of abridging and isolating Lincoln's words has had the effect of distorting history. Cited alone, Lincoln's statement on labor unions sounds like approval, "I am glad to see that a system of labor prevails in New England under which laborers can strike when they want to." But in truth these words were mocking and followed by "I like the system that lets a man quit when he wants to, and wish it might prevail everywhere."

Needless to say this book is not an exhaustive compilation of Lincoln quotes, nor a scholarly study of their authenticity and possible sources. Our only intention is to sketch, with the color, clarity, and shape of his own words, a small, pocket-size portrait of the living Abraham Lincoln.

Thanks to Mr. Lincoln for his wisdom,
his strength, his sense of humor.
Thanks also to Pete and Tom.
And, of course, to Lefty,
the best four-legged agent in New York.

LINCOLN ON LINCOLN

I am, in height, six feet four inches, nearly; lean in flesh, weighing on average one hundred and eighty pounds; dark complexion, with coarse black hair and grey eyes. No other marks or brands recollected.

> [To the compiler of *The Dictionary of Congress*] Born February 12, 1809, in Hardin County, Kentucky. Education defective. Profession, a lawyer. Have been a captain of volunteers in Black Hawk War. Postmaster at a very small office. Four times a member of the Illinois Legislature and was a member of the lower house of Congress.
>
> Yours, etc. A. Lincoln.

As you are all so anxious for me to distinguish myself, I have concluded to do so before long.

It is a great piece of folly to attempt to make anything out of me or my early life. It can all be condensed into a single sentence, and that sentence you will find in Gray's *Elegy [in a Country Churchyard]:* "The short and simple annals of the poor." That's my life, and that's all you or anyone can make out of it.

I was not much accustomed to flattery, and it came the sweeter to me. I was rather like the Hoosier with the gingerbread, when he said he reckoned he loved it better than any other man, and got less of it.

If elected I shall be thankful; if not, it will be all the same.

Nobody has ever expected me to be President. In my poor, lean, lank face nobody has ever seen that any cabbages were sprouting.

I shall do nothing in malice. What I deal with is too vast for malicious dealing.

I cannot but know what you all know, that without a name, perhaps without a reason why I should have a name, there has fallen upon me a task such as did not rest even upon the Father of this Country.

[On requests that he revoke the Emancipation Proclamation]

. . . a cruel and astounding breach of faith [for which] I should be damned in time and eternity. . . . The world shall know that I will keep my faith to friends and enemies, come what will.

The race gave me a hearing on the great and durable question of the age, which I could have had in no other way; and though I now sink out of view, and shall be forgotten, I believe I have made some marks which will tell for the cause of civil liberty long after I am gone.

[Recalling his Second Inaugural Address on the war's imminent end, "Malice Toward None, Charity for All"] Lots of wisdom in that document I suspect . . . [it would] wear as well as—perhaps better than—anything . . . but I believe it is not immediately popular.

At least I should have done my duty, and have stood clear before my own conscience.

I have said nothing but what I am willing to live by, and, if it be the pleasure of Almighty God, to die by.

Die when I may, I want it said of me that I plucked a weed and planted a flower wherever I thought a flower would grow.

On the American Dream

You can better your condition, and so it may go on and on and on in one ceaseless round so long as man exists on the face of the earth!

There is no permanent class of hired laborers amongst us. Twenty-five years ago, I was a hired laborer. The hired laborer of yesterday, labors on his own account today; and will hire others to labor for him tomorrow. Advancement—improvement in condition—is the order of things in a society of equals.

I am not ashamed to confess that twenty-five years ago I was a hired laborer, mauling rails, at work on a flat-boat—just what might happen to any poor man's son. I want every man to have a chance—and I believe a black man is entitled to it—in which he can better his condition—when he may look forward and hope to be a hired laborer this year and the next, work for himself afterward, and finally to hire men to work for him! That is the true system.

I hold the value of life is to improve one's condition. Whatever is calculated to advance the condition of the honest, struggling, laboring man, so far as my judgment will enable me to judge of a correct thing, I am for that thing.

[Lincoln recalls how, as a boy, he was struck while reading about Christmas Night of 1776 in Parson Weem's account *Life of Washington*. This was the night George Washington led the Revolutionary Army through a sleet storm across the Delaware River.]
I recollect thinking then, boy even though I was, that there must have been something more than common that those men struggled for . . . something even more than National Independence . . . something that held out a great promise to all the people of the world for all time to come . . . promise that in due time the weights should be lifted from the shoulders of all men, and that *all* should have an equal chance. . . . If this country cannot be saved without giving up that principle, I was about to say I would rather be assassinated on this spot than surrender it.

On the side of the Union it is a struggle for maintaining in the world that form and substance of government whose leading object is to elevate the condition of men . . . to afford all an unfettered start, and a fair chance in the race of life.

Thanks to all. For the great republic—for the principle it lives by, and keeps alive—for man's vast future—thanks to all.

On Acquired Taste

[Asked his opinion on a very sentimental book]
People who like this sort of thing will find this the sort of thing they like.

He has a right to criticize, who has a heart to help.

I can truthfully say that the painter has observed the Ten Commandments. Because he hath not made to himself the likeness of anything in heaven above, or that which is on earth beneath, or that which is in the water under the earth.

[In conversation with a popular singer]

Lincoln: "I think I might become a musician if I heard you often, but so far I know only two tunes."

The singer: " 'Hail Columbia'? You know that, I am sure."

Lincoln: "Oh, yes; I know that; for I have to stand up and take off my hat."

The singer: "And the other one?"

Lincoln: "The other one? Oh, the other one is the other when I don't stand up."

ON THE ALMIGHTY DOLLAR

Money is only valuable while in circulation . . .

These capitalists generally act harmoniously and in concert, to fleece the people, and now, that they have got into a quarrel with themselves, we are called upon to appropriate the people's money to settle the quarrel.

It is an old maxim and a very sound one that he that dances should always pay the fiddler. . . . I am decidedly opposed to the people's money being used to pay the fiddler.

The plainest print cannot be read through a gold eagle.

Moral principle is a looser bond than pecuniary interest.

Protect labor against the evils of a vicious currency, and facilitate commerce by cheap and safe exchanges.

[Response to Secretary of the Treasury, Salmon P. Chase, who insisted that printing paper money to pay the troops because of silver and gold shortages was unconstitutional]
You take care of the Treasury and I will take care of the Constitution.

That some should be rich, shows that others may become rich, and, hence, is just encouragement to industry and enterprise.

ON TAXES

The objection of paying arises from the want of ability to pay.

I go for all sharing the privileges of the government who assist in bearing its burthens.

Doubtless some of those who are to pay, and not to receive, will object [to taxation].

If we should wait before collecting a tax, to adjust the taxes upon each man in exact proportion with every other man, we should never collect any tax at all.

ON COMMERCE

Unless among those deficient of intellect, everybody you trade with makes something.

If you make a bad bargain, hug it all the tighter.

ON AMBITION

I have never professed an indifference to the honors of official station; and were I to do so now, I should only make myself ridiculous.

The proudest ambition he could desire was to do something for the elevation of the condition of his fellow man.

Every man is said to have his particular ambition. Whether it be true or not, I can say for one that I have no other so great as that of being truly esteemed of my fellow men . . .

Will springs from the two elements of moral sense and self-interest.

It is not in the nature of man to be driven to anything; still less to be driven about that which is exclusively his own business; and least of all where such driving is to be submitted to at the expense of pecuniary interest or burning appetite.

Men are not flattered by being shown that there has been a difference of purpose between the Almighty and them.

It can truly be said of him that while he was personally ambitious, he bravely endured the obscurity which the unpopularity of his principle imposed, and never accepted official honors, until those honors were ready to admit his principles with him.

At every step we must be true to the main purpose.

. . . with the catching, end the pleasures of the chase.

Always bear in mind that your own resolution to succeed is more important than any other one thing.

ON ANSWERING TO CRITICS

I have endured a great deal of ridicule without much malice; and have received a great deal of kindness, not quite free from ridicule. I am used to it.

When a man hears himself somewhat misrepresented, it provokes him—at least, I find it so with myself; but when misrepresentation becomes very gross and palpable, it is more apt to amuse him.

It is not entirely safe, when one is misrepresented under his very nose, to allow the misrepresentation to go uncorrected.

If I were to try to read, much less answer, all the attacks made on me, this shop might as well be closed for any other business. I do the very best I know how—the very best I can; and I mean to keep doing so until the end. If the end brings me out all right, what is said against me won't amount to anything. If the end brings me out wrong, ten angels swearing I was right would make no difference.

On Burying the Hatchet

Am I not destroying my enemies when I make friends of them?

With malice toward none; with charity for all; with firmness in the right, let us strive on to finish the work we are in; to bind up the nation's wounds; to care for him who shall have borne the battle, and for his widow, and his orphan—to do all which may achieve and cherish a just and lasting peace, among ourselves, and with all nations.

Let bygones be bygones; let past differences as nothing be; and with steady eye on the real issue, let us reinaugurate the good old "central ideas" of the republic. The human heart is with us. God is with us.

I entertain no unkind feeling to you, and none of any sort upon the subject, except a sincere regret that I permitted myself to get into such an altercation.

On principle I dislike an oath which requires a man to swear he has not done wrong. It rejects the Christian principle of forgiveness on terms of repentance. I think it is enough if the man does no wrong hereafter.

[Asked by a priest to suspend the sentence of a man ordered put to death]
If I don't suspend it tonight, the man will surely be suspended tomorrow.

We must not be enemies. Though passion may have strained, it must not break our bonds of affection. The mystic chords of memory, stretching from every battlefield, and patriot grave, to every living heart and hearthstone, all over this broad land, will yet swell the chorus of the Union, when again touched, as surely they will be, by the better angels of our nature.

Blood can not restore blood, and government should not act for revenge . . .

The spirit of concession and compromise—that spirit which has never failed us in past perils, and which may be safely trusted for all the future.

I wish you to do nothing merely for revenge, but that what you may do shall be solely done with reference to the security of the future.

I will pardon Jeff Davis, if he asks for it.

Yield larger things to which you can show no more than equal right; and yield lesser ones, though clearly your own. Better give your path to a dog, than be bitten by him in contesting for the right. Even killing the dog would not cure the bite.

We can succeed only by concert. It is not "Can any of us imagine better?" but, "Can we all do better?"

On Civil Liberties

The cause of civil liberty must not be surrendered at the end of *one,* or even one *hundred* defeats.

Must a government of necessity, be too *strong* for the liberties of its own people, or too *weak* to maintain its own existence?

I can no more be persuaded that the government can constitutionally take no strong measure in time of rebellion, because it can be shown that the same could not be lawfully taken in time of peace, that I can be persuaded that a particular drug is not good medicine for a sick man, because it can be shown to not be good food for a well one.

By general law life *and* limb must be protected; yet often a limb must be amputated to save a life; but a life is never wisely given to save a limb.

I have been unwilling to go beyond the pressure of necessity in the unusual exercise of power.

More rogues than honest men find shelter under habeas corpus.

Nor am I able to appreciate the danger . . . that the American people will, by means of military arrests during the rebellion, lose the right of public discussion, the liberty of speech and the press, the law of evidence, trial by jury, and habeas corpus, throughout the indefinite peaceful future which I trust lies before them, any more than I am able to believe that a man could contract so strong an appetite for emetics in feeding upon temporary illness, as to persist in feeding upon them through the remainder of his healthful life.

Nothing in the Constitution or laws of any state can destroy a right distinctly and expressly affirmed in the Constitution of the United States.

Don't interfere with anything in the Constitution. That must be maintained, for it is the only safeguard of our liberties.

The right of peaceable assembly and of petition . . . is the constitutional substitute for revolution.

If destruction be our lot we must ourselves be its author and finisher. As a nation of freemen we must live through all time, or die by suicide.

That our principle [freedom & equality], however baf-
fled, or delayed, will finally triumph, I do not permit
myself to doubt. Men will pass away—die—die, politically and naturally; but the principle will live, and live
forever.

On the Courts

It is a maxim held by the courts, that there is no wrong
without its remedy; and the courts have a remedy for
whatever is acknowledged and treated as a wrong.

Some other things I have fears for. I am not easy about
the Courts. I am satisfied with them as they are; but
shall care much if the judges are made elective by the
People, and their terms of office limited.

I fear . . . "A Puppy Court" . . . "A Migratory [state]
Supreme Court" and Salaries so low as to exclude all re-
spectable talent. From these, may God preserve us.

I grant you that an unconstitutional act is not a law; but
I do not ask and will not take your construction of the
Constitution. The Supreme Court of the United States

is the tribunal to decide such questions, and we will submit to its decisions . . .

We think its decisions on constitutional questions, when fully settled, should control, not only the particular cases decided, but the general policy of the country, subject to be disturbed only by amendments of the Constitution as provided in that instrument itself.

[On the *Dred Scott* decision (1857)]
If this important decision had been made by the unanimous concurrence of the judges, and without any apparent partisan bias, and in accordance with legal public expectation, and with the steady practice of the departments throughout our history, and had been in no wanting in some of these, it had been before the court more than once, and had there been affirmed and reaffirmed through a course of years, it then might be, perhaps would be, factious, nay, even revolutionary, to not acquiesce in it as a precedent.

Judicial decisions are of greater of less authority as precedents, according to circumstances. That this should be so accords both with common sense and the customary understanding of the legal profession.

But no organic law can ever be framed with a provision specifically applicable to every question which may occur in practical administration. No firesight can anticipate, nor any document of reasonable length contain express provisions for all possible questions.

Legislation and adjudication must follow, and conform to, the progress of society.

On Faith &
Redemption

My concern is not whether God is on our side; my great concern is to be on God's side.

How true it is that "God tempers the wind to the shorn lamb," or in other words, that He renders the worst of human conditions tolerable, while He permits the best to be nothing better than tolerable.

If we do right God will be with us, and if God is with us we cannot fail.

Men are not flattered by being shown that there has been a difference of purpose between the Almighty and them.

Let us have faith that right makes might; and in that faith let us to the end dare to do our duty as we understand it.

That I am not the member of any Christian Church, is true; but I have never denied the truth of the Scriptures; and I have never spoken with intentional disrespect of religion in general, or of any denomination of Christians in particular.

I have often wished that I was a more devout man than I am.

You say your husband is a religious man; tell him when you meet him, that I say I am not much of a judge of religion, but that, in my opinion, the religion that sets men to rebel and fight against their government, because, as they think, that government does not sufficiently help some men to eat their bread on the sweat of other men's faces, is not the sort of religion upon which people can get to heaven!

If it is probable that God would reveal His will to others on a point so connected with my duty, it might be supposed He would reveal it directly to me.

Certainly there is no contending against the will of God, but still there is some difficulty in ascertaining it, and applying it, to particular cases.

The Bible . . . The best gift God has given to man.

The Bible says somewhere that we are desperately self-ish. I think we would have discovered that fact without the Bible.

Leaving the matter of eternal consequences, between him and his Maker, I still do not think any man has the right thus to insult the feelings, and injure the morals, of the community in which he may live.

Without the assistance of that Divine Being who ever attended him, I cannot succeed. With that assistance I cannot fail. Trusting in Him who can go with me, and remain with you, and be everywhere for good, let us confidently hope that all will yet be well.

On Fellowship

The better part of one's life consists in his friendships.

I am slow to listen to criminations among friends, and never espouse their quarrels on either side. My sincere wish is that both sides will allow bygones to be bygones, and look to the present and future only.

The inclination to exchange thoughts with one another is probably an original impulse of our nature.

Of all things, avoid if possible, a dividing into cliques among the friends of the common object.

"A drop of honey catches more flies than a gallon of gall." So with men. If you would win a man to your cause, first convince him that you are his sincere friend. Therein is a drop of honey which catches his heart, which, say what he will, is the great highroad to reason.

The loss of enemies does not compensate for the loss of friends.

Let us at all times remember that all American citizens are brothers of a common country, and should dwell together in the bonds of fraternal feeling.

On Government by the People

This country, with its institutions, belongs to the people who inhabit it. Whenever they shall grow weary of the existing government, they can exercise their constitutional right of amending it, or their revolutionary right to dismember or overthrow it.

No man is good enough to govern another man, without that other's consent, I say this is the leading principle—the sheet anchor of American republicanism.

He [Senator Douglas] discovered that the right to breed and flog Negroes in Nebraska was popular sovereignty.

I think a definition of "popular sovereignty" in the abstract, would be about this: That each man shall do precisely as he pleases with himself, and with all those things that exclusively concern him . . . that a general government shall do all those things which pertain to it, and all the local governments shall do precisely as they please in respect to those matters which exclusively concern them.

. . . we here highly resolve that these dead shall not have died in vain; that this nation, under God, shall have a new birth of freedom; and that government of the people, by the people, for the people, shall not perish from the earth.

The most reliable indication of public purpose in this country is derived through our popular elections.

Our government rests in public opinion. Whoever can change public opinion can change the government.

To give the victory to the right, not bloody bullets, but peaceful ballots only are necessary. Thanks to our good old Constitution, and organization under it, these alone are necessary. It only needs that every right thinking man shall go to the polls, and without fear or prejudice vote as he thinks.

It is not the qualified voters, but the qualified voters who choose to vote, that constitute the political power of the State.

Among free men there can be no successful appeal from the ballot to the bullet, and they who take such appeal are sure to lose their case and pay the cost.

I reiterate that the majority should rule. If I adopt a wrong policy, the opportunity for condemnation will occur in four years' time. Then I can be turned out, and a better man with better views put in my place.

When the white man governs himself, that is self-government; but when he governs himself and also governs another man, that is more than self-government—that is despotism.

Any people anywhere, being inclined and having the power, have the right to rise up and shake off their existing government, and form a new one that suits them better. This is a most valuable, a most sacred right—a right which we hope and believe is to liberate the world.

———

If there is anything which it is the duty of the whole people to never intrust to any hands but their own, that thing is the preservation and perpetuity of their own liberties and institutions.

What is "sovereignty" in the political sense of the term? Would it be far wrong to define it a "political community without a political superior?"

In this age, and in this country, public sentiment is everything. With it, nothing can fail; against it, nothing can succeed.

Public opinion is founded, to a great extent, on a property basis. What lessens the value of property is opposed, what enhances its value is favored.

The public interest and my private interest have been, perfectly parallel, because in no other way could I serve myself so well, as by truly serving the Union.

A universal feeling, whether well or ill-founded, cannot be safely disregarded.

———

On His Good Looks

Common looking people are the best in the world: that is the reason the Lord makes so many of them.

[Asked about a photograph he posed for]
Well, I must say, as my grandfather did when he saw his daguerreotype: "It's most horribly like me."

[Asked about the irreality of artists' renderings]
It is impossible to get my graceful motions in—that's the reason why none of the pictures are like me.

[Asked how long a man's legs should be in proportion to his body]
I have not given the matter much consideration, but on first blush I should judge they ought to be long enough to reach from his body to the ground.

[Responding to a friend who commented that his coat was too short in the waist]
Never mind; it'll be long enough before I get another!

[Asked why he walked so crookedly]
Oh, my nose, you see, is crooked, and I have to follow it!

[Getting a laugh at an Illinois convention of Republican editors]
I feel like I once did when I met a woman riding horseback in the woods. As I stopped to let her pass, she also stopped, and looking at me intently, said: "I do believe you are the ugliest man I ever saw." Said I: "Madam, you are probably right, but I can't help it!" "No," said she, "you can't help it, but you could stay home."

[To a woman who wanted to get a look at the president]
Well, in the matter of looking at one another, I have altogether the advantage.

ON HONESTY AS GOOD POLICY

I never encourage deceit, and falsehood, especially if you have got a bad memory, is the worst enemy a fellow can have. The fact is, truth is your truest friend, no matter what the circumstances are.

If I were two-faced, would I be wearing this one?

Let the people know the truth and country is safe.

Truth is generally the best vindication against slander.

> Question: How many legs does a dog have if you call the tail a leg?
> Answer: Four. Calling a tail a leg doesn't make it a leg.

On Life's Joys & Sorrows

People are just about as happy as they make up their minds to be.

It is difficult to make a man miserable while he feels he is worthy of himself and claims kindred to the great God who made him.

Remember that in the depth and even the agony of despondency, that very shortly you are to feel well again.

There is but one thing about her, so far as I could perceive, that I would have otherwise than as it is. That is something of a tendency to melancholy. This, let it be observed, is a misfortune not a fault.

In this sad world of ours, sorrow comes to all; and, to the young, it comes with bitterest agony, because it takes them unawares. The older have learned to ever expect it.

[For a childhood acquaintance who went insane at age nineteen]

> *Here's an object of more dread*
> *Than aught the grave contains—*
> *A human form with reason fled,*
> *While wretched life remains.*

[Asked how he felt after the Democrats won the New York elections]
Somewhat like the boy in Kentucky who stubbed his toe while running to see his sweetheart. The boy said he was too big to cry, and far too badly hurt to laugh.

As the proverb goes, no man knows so well where the shoe pinches as he who wears it.

[From a letter of condolence]
I am sorry now to be the author of the slightest pain to you. But I was in such deep distress myself that I could not restrain some expression of it.

Problems. The smallest are often the most difficult to deal with.

I would rather meet [problems] *as* they come, than *before* they come, trusting that some of them may not come at all.

If the good people, in their wisdom, shall see fit to keep me in the background, I have been too familiar with disappointments to be very much chagrined.

[On reaction to the Emancipation Proclamation, reading it for the first time to cabinet members]
Read it through, and there was dead silence. Then Mr. Chase spoke and said he liked all but so and so, then someone else made an objection, and then another, until all had said something. Then I said: "Gentlemen, this reminds me of the story of the man who had been away from home, and when he was coming back was met by one of his farm hands, who greeted him after this fashion: 'Master, the little pigs are dead, and the old sow's dead, too, but I didn't like to tell you all at once.' "

It is said an Eastern monarch once charged his wise men to invent him an aphorism to be ever in view, and which should be true and appropriate in all times and situations. They presented him the words, "And this, too, shall pass away."

On Labor

The strongest bond of human sympathy, outside of the family relation, should be one uniting all working people, of all nations, and tongues, and kindreds.

Few can be induced to labor exclusively for posterity; and none will do it enthusiastically.

If the Almighty had ever made a set of men that should do all the eating and none of the work, He would have made them with mouths only and no hands.

The working people are the basis of all government, for the plain reason that they are the most numerous.

An honest laborer digs coal at about seventy cents a day, while the President digs abstractions at about seventy dollars a day. The coal is clearly worth more than the abstractions, and yet what a monstrous inequality in the prices.

Inasmuch as most good things are produced by labor, it follows that all such things of right belong to those whose labor has produced them. But it has so happened, in all ages of the world, that some have labored, and others have without labor enjoyed a large proportion of the fruits. This is wrong, and should not continue. To secure to each laborer the whole product of his labor, or as nearly as possible, is a worthy subject of any good government.

Free labor has the inspiration of hope; pure slavery has no hope. The power of hope upon human exertion and happiness is wonderful.

As labor is the common burden of our race, so the effort of some to shift their share of the burden onto the shoulders of others is the great durable curse of the race.

Property is the fruit of labor—property is desirable—is a positive good in the world.

I am glad to see that a system of labor prevails in New England under which laborers can strike when they want to . . . I like the system that lets a man quit when he wants to, and wish it might prevail everywhere.

You say you would at most give your place in heaven for seventy or eighty dollars. Then you value your place in heaven very cheap, for I am sure you can, with the offer I make, get seventy or eighty dollars for four of five months' work.

Labor is prior to, and independent of, capital. Capital is only the fruit of labor, and could never have existed if labor had not first existed. Labor is the superior of capital, and deserves much the higher consideration.

On Land & Prosperity

I take it that it is best for all to leave each man free to acquire property as fast as he can. Some will get wealthy. I don't believe in a law to prevent a man from getting rich; it would do more harm than good.

Part with the land you have, and, my life upon it, you will never after own a spot big enough to bury you in.

He desired the prosperity of his countrymen partly because they were his countrymen, but chiefly to show to the world that freemen could be prosperous.

Sad evidence that, feeling prosperity, we forget right . . .

Let us hope . . . that by the best cultivation of the physical world, beneath and around us, and the intellectual and moral world within us, we shall secure an individual, social and political prosperity and happiness, whose course shall be onward and upward, and which, while the earth endures, shall not pass away.

I wish all men to be free. I wish the material prosperity of the already free [extended to all] which I feel sure the extinction of slavery would bring.

On Law-Abiding
Citizens

Let every man remember that to violate the law is to trample on the blood of his father, and to tear the charter of his own and his children's liberty.

No law is stronger than is the public sentiment where it is to be enforced.

It is as much the duty of government to render prompt justice against itself, in favor of citizens, as it is to administer the same between private individuals.

Why should their not be a patient confidence in the ultimate justice of the people? Is there any better or equal hope in the world?

Let not him who is houseless pull down the house of another, but let him work diligently and build one for himself, thus by example assuring that his own shall be safe from violence when built.

Can aliens make treaties easier than friends can make

laws? Can treaties be more faithfully enforced between aliens than laws can among friends?

Let reverence for the laws be breathed by every American mother to the lisping babe that prattles on her lap; let it be taught in schools, in seminaries, and in colleges; let it be written in Primers, spelling books, and in Almanacs; let it be preached from the pulpit, proclaimed in legislative halls, and enforced in courts of justice. And, in short, let it become the *political religion* of the nation; and let the old and the young, the rich and the poor, the grave and the gay, of all sexes and tongues, and colors and conditions, sacrifice unceasingly upon its altars.

. . . bad laws, if they exist, should be repealed as soon as possible, still while they continue in force, for the sake of example, they should be religiously observed.

A jury too frequently has at least one member more ready to hang the panel than to hang the traitor.

A law may be both constitutional and expedient, and yet may be administered in an unjust and unfair way.

The severst justice may not always be the best policy.

On Lawyers

Resolve to be honest at all events; and if in your own judgment you cannot be an honest lawyer, resolve to be honest without being a lawyer.

I have sometimes seen a good lawyer, struggling for his client's neck in a desperate case, employing every artifice to work round, befog and cover up with many words some point arising in the case which he *dared* not admit and yet *could* not deny.

Discourage litigation. Persuade your neighbor to compromise whenever you can. Point out to them how the nominal winner is often a real loser—in fees, expenses, and waste of time. As a peacemaker the lawyer has a superior opportunity of being a good man. There will still be business enough.

In law it is good policy to never *plead* what you *need* not, lest you oblige yourself to *prove* what you *can* not.

That *is* good book-law; but is not the rule of actual practice.

I understand that it is a maxim of law, that a poor plea may be a good plea to a bad declaration.

There is a vague popular belief that lawyers are necessarily dishonest. I say vague, because when we consider to what extent confidence and honors are reposed in and conferred upon lawyers by the people, it appears improbable that their impression of dishonesty is very distinct and vivid.

Whatever fees we [Judge Logan and I] earn at a distance, if not paid *before*, we notice we never hear of after the work is done. We therefore, are growing a little sensitive on the point.

Extemporaneous speaking should be practiced and cultivated. It is the lawyer's avenue to the public. However able and faithful he may be in other respects, people are slow to bring him business if he cannot make a speech. And yet there is not a more fatal error to young lawyers than relying too much on speech-making. If any one, upon his rare powers of speaking, shall claim an exemption from the drudgery of the law, his case is a failure in advance.

ON STRONG LEADERSHIP

He who does *something* at the head of one regiment, will eclipse him who does *nothing* at the head of a hundred.

The man who stands by and says nothing when the peril of his government is discussed, cannot be misunderstood. If not hindered, he is sure to help the enemy; much more if he talks ambiguously—talks for his country with "ifs" and "ands" and "buts."

I claim not to have controlled events, but confess plainly that events have controlled me.

I think the necessity of being *ready* increases. Look to it.

Tell him, when he starts, to put it through—not to be writing or telegraphing back here, but put it through.

I am a slow walker, but I do not walk backward.

As our case is new, so we must think anew, and act anew.

———

Important principles may, and must, be flexible.

[To criticism that he changed his mind]
Yes I have; and I don't think much of a man who is not wiser today than yesterday.

I shall do less whenever I shall believe what I am doing hurts the cause, and I shall do more whenever I shall believe doing more will help the cause. I shall try to correct errors when shown to be errors; and I shall adopt new views so fast as they shall appear to be true views.

"Do nothing at all, lest you do something wrong" is the sum of these positions . . .

What is conservatism? Is it not adherence to the old and untried, against the new and untried?

The dogmas of the quiet past are inadequate to the stormy present.

I hope to "stand firm" enough not to go backward, and yet not go forward fast enough to wreck the country's cause.

———

If you once forfeit the confidence of your fellow citizens, you can never regain their respect and esteem. It is true that you may fool all the people some of the time; you can even fool some of the people all the time; but you can't fool all of the people all the time.

Stand on middle ground and hold the ship level and steady.

How to do something and still not do too much is the desideratum.

For my own views, I have not offered and do not now offer them as orders; and while I am glad to have them respectfully considered, I would blame you to follow them contrary to your own dear judgment—unless I should put them in the form of orders.

It is the duty of nations as well as of men to own their dependence upon the overruling power of God.

ON NORTH & SOUTH

We know that some Southern men do free their slaves, go North and become tip-top Abolitionists, while some

Northern ones go South and become cruel slave-masters.

The rebel soldiers are praying with a great deal more earnestness, I fear, than our own troops, and expecting God to favor their side; for one of our soldiers . . . said that he met with nothing so discouraging as the evident sincerity of those he was among in their prayers.

As I have not felt, so I have not expressed any harsh sentiment towards our Southern brethren. I have constantly declared, as I really believed, the only difference between them and us, is the difference of circumstances.

One side ignored the *necessity*, and magnified the evils of the system; while the other ignored the evils and magnified the necessity; and each bitterly assailed the motives of the other.

Both parties deprecated war; but one of them would *make* war rather than let the nation survive; and the other would *accept* war rather than let it perish. And the war came.

The Constitution is as silent about that, as it is silent personally about myself.

I have always thought the act of secession is legally nothing, and needs no repealing.

In considering the policy to be adopted for suppressing the insurrection, I have been anxious and careful that the inevitable conflict for this purpose shall not degenerate into a violent and remorseless revolutionary struggle.

. . . the right of revolution, is never a legal right. . . . At most, it is but a moral right, when exercised for a morally justifiable cause. When exercised without such a cause revolution is no right, but simply a wicked exercise of physical power.

Let me say right here that only the unanimous consent of the states can dissolve this Union.

On Politics

ON FINE STATESMEN

Men of the speaking sort of talent.

This work is exclusively the work of politicians; a set of men who have interests aside from the interests of the people, and who, to say the most of them, are, taken as a mass, at least one long step removed from honest men. I say this with the greater freedom because, being a politician myself, none can regard it as personal.

[On another member of the Illinois Legislature]
In one faculty, at least, there can be no dispute of the gentleman's superiority over me, and most other men; and that is, the faculty of entangling a subject, so that neither himself, nor any other man can find head or tail to it.

[On Stephen A. Douglas]
His argument is as thin as the homeopathic soup that was made by boiling the shadow of a pigeon that had been starved to death.

You violated the primary, the cardinal, the one great living principle of all democratic representative government—the principle that the representative is bound to carry out the known will of his constituents.

ON PATRONAGE AND PORK BARREL DEALS

Too many pigs; two few teats.

[A recommendation for appointment]
Mr. Bond I know to be, personally, every way worthy of the office; and he is very numerously and most respectably recommended. His paper I send to you; and I solicit for his claims a full and fair consideration. Having said this much, I add that, in my individual judgment, the appointment of Mr. Thomas would be better.

Not knowing whether he [Charles Wiegand] is fit for any place, I could not with propriety recommend him for any.

Were it believed that vacant places could be had at the North Pole, the road there would be lined with dead Virginians.

[To a Democratic congressman who inquired after a minor appointment for one of his constituents]

That reminds me of my own experience as an Old Whig member of Congress. I was always in the opposition, and I had no troubles of this kind at all. It was the easiest thing imaginable to be an opposition member—no running to the departments and the White House.

ON PARTY POLITICS

No party can command respect which sustains this year what it opposed the last.

In the absence of formal written platforms, the antecedents of candidates become their platforms. On just such platforms all our earlier and better Presidents were elected.

The process is this: Three, four, or half a dozen questions are prominent at a given time; the party selects its candidate, and he takes his position on each of these questions. On all but one his positions have already been endorsed at former elections, and his party fully committed to them; but that one is new, and a large portion of them are against it. But what are they to do? The whole are strung together, and they must take all or reject all. They cannot take what they like and reject the rest. What they are already committed to, being the majority, they shut their eyes and gulp the whole.

If any of us allow ourselves to seek out minor or separate points on which there may be difference of views as to policy and right... [that will] keep us from uniting in action upon a great principle in a cause on which we all agree...

Merely settlements of small phases of the question, not of the question itself.

Unanimity is possible.

[On party conventions]
I think too much reliance is placed in noisy demonstrations, importing speakers from a distance and the like. They excite prejudice and close the avenues to sober reason. The "home production" principle in my judgment is the best.

ON THE REPUBLICAN PARTY

We [Republicans] have to fight this battle upon principle alone, so I hope those with whom I am surrounded have principle enough to nerve themselves for the task, and leave nothing undone that can fairly be done to bring about the right result.

The only danger will be the temptation to lower the Republican Standards in order to gather recruits. In my judgment such a step would be a serious mistake— would open a gap through which more would pass *out* than pass *in*.

We hold the true Republican position. In leaving the people's business in their hands, we cannot be wrong.

ON CAMPAIGNS

I would despise myself if I thought that I was procuring your votes by concealing my opinions, and by avowing one set of principles in one part of the state and a different set in another.

I do not allow myself to suppose that either the Convention or the League have concluded to decide that I am either the greatest or the best man in America, but rather they have concluded it is not best to swap horses while crossing the river, and have further concluded that I am not so poor a horse and that they might not make a botch of it in trying to swap.

My name is new in the field, and I suppose I am not the first choice of a great many. Our policy then is to give no offense to others—leave them in a mood to come to us if they shall be compelled to give up their first love.

You suggest that a visit to the place of my nativity [Kentucky] might be pleasant to me. Indeed it would. But would it be safe? Would not the people lynch me?

The strife of the election is but human nature practically applied to the facts of the case.

Yes, sir, that [military] coat tail was used, not only for General Jackson himself, but has been clung to with the grip of death by every Democratic candidate since. . . . A fellow once advertised that he had made a discovery, by which he could make a new man out of an old one, and have enough of the stuff left to make a little yellow dog. Just such a discovery has General Jackson's popularity been to you. You not only twice made President of him out of it, but you have had enough of the stuff left to make Presidents of several comparatively small men since.

It seems exceedingly probable that this administration will not be reelected. Then it will be my duty to cooperate with the President-elect, as to save the Union between the election and the inauguration, as he will have secured his election on such ground that he cannot possibly save it afterward.

ON POLITICS AND DOLLARS

I say, in the main, the use of money is wrong; but for certain objects in a political contest, the use of some is both right and indispensable.

I cannot enter the ring on the money basis—first, because, in the main, it is wrong; and secondly, I have not, and can not get, the money.

I could not raise ten thousand dollars if it would save me from the fate of John Brown. Nor have my friends, so far as I know, yet reached the point of staking any money on my chances of success.

On the Presidency of the United States

The Presidency, even to the most experienced politicians, is no bed of roses . . .

No human being can fill that station and escape censure.

I am responsible . . . to the American people, to the Christian world, to history, and on my final account to God.

I have been told I was on the road to Hell, but I had no idea it was just a mile down the road with a dome on it.

My policy is to have no policy.

To throw the responsibility . . . is fixing for the President the unjust and ruinous character of being a mere man of straw. This must be arrested, or it will damn us all inevitably. . . . He must occasionally say, or seem to say, by the Eternal, "I take responsibility." Those phrases were the "Samson's locks" of Gen. [Andrew] Jackson, and we dare not disregard the lessons of experience.

Remembering that when not a very great man begins to be mentioned for a very great position, his head is very likely to be a little turned, I concluded I am not the fittest person to answer the questions you ask.

The taste *is* in my mouth a little; and this, no doubt, disqualifies me, to some extent, to form correct opinions.

Were I president, I should desire the legislation of the country to rest with Congress, uninfluenced by the executive in its origin or progress, and undisturbed by the veto unless in very special and clear cases.

I should have been selected to fill an important office for a brief period. . . . Should my administration prove to be a very wicked one, or what is more probable, a very foolish one, if you the PEOPLE are but true to yourselves and to the Constitution, there is but little harm I can do, *thank God!*

. . . if you remain true and honest, you cannot be betrayed. My power is temporary; yours as eternal as the principles of liberty.

I freely acknowledge myself the servant of the people.

[On Thomas Jefferson]
Was, is, and perhaps will continue to be, the most distinguished politician of our history.

I bring to the work an honest heart; I dare not tell you that I bring a head sufficient for it.

I have not permitted myself, gentleman, to conclude that I am the best man in the country; but I am reminded, in this connection, of a story of an old Dutch farmer, who remarked to a companion once that "it was not best to swap horses when crossing streams."

I must in candor say I do not think myself fit for the presidency.

[Asked by an old friend from Illinois how he liked being President]
You have heard the story, haven't you, about the man as was ridden out of town on a rail, tarred and feathered, somebody asked him how he liked it, and his reply was if it was not for the honor of the thing, he would very much rather walk.

As a pilot I have used my best exertions to keep afloat our Ship of State, and shall be glad to resign my trust at the appointed time to another pilot more skillful and successful than I may prove.

I desire to conduct the affairs of this administration that if at the end, when I come to lay down the reins of power, I have lost every other friend on earth, I shall at least have one friend left, and that friend shall be down inside me.

On Progress

A new country is most favorable—almost necessary—to the emancipation of thought, and the consequent advancement of civilization and the arts.

Very much like stopping a skiff in the middle of a river—if it was not going up, it *would* go down.

Without the Constitution and the Union, we could not have attained the result; but even these are not the primary cause of our great prosperity. There is something back of these, entwining itself more closely about the human heart. That something is the principle of "Liberty to all"—the principle that clears the *path* for all—gives *hope* to all—and, by consequence, *enterprise*, and *industry* to all.

Towering genius disdains a beaten path. It seeks regions hitherto unexplored.

Our thanks, and something more substantial than thanks, are due to the man engaged in the effort to produce a successful steam plow.

On Readin' & Writin'

Upon the subject of education, not presuming to dictate any plan or system respecting it, I can only say that

I view it as the most important subject which we as a people may be engaged in. That everyone may receive at least a moderate education appears to be an objective of vital importance.

No qualification was ever required of a teacher beyond "readin', writin', and cipherin' " to the rule of three. If a straggler supposed to understand Latin happened to sojourn in the neighborhood, he was looked upon as a wizard.

[Response to the comment, "It may be doubted whether any man of our generation has plunged more deeply into the sacred fount of learning"]
Or come up drier.

Writing, the art of communicating thoughts to the mind through the eye, is the great invention of the world . . . enabling us to converse with the dead, the absent, and the unborn, at all distances of time and space.

At length printing came. It gave ten thousand copies of any written matter, quite as cheaply as ten were given before; and consequently a thousand minds were brought into the field where there was but one before.

Printing . . . is but the *other* half—and in real utility, the *better* half—of writing; and that both together are but the assistants of speech in the communication of thoughts between man and man.

A capacity, and taste, for reading, gives access to whatever has already been discovered by others. It is the key, or one of the keys, to the already solved problems.

On Shifting Blame

I surely will not blame them for not doing what I should not know how to do myself.

We cannot ask a man what he will do, and if we should, and he should answer us, we should despise him for it. Therefore, we must take a man whose opinions are known.

So ready are we all to cry out, and ascribe motives, when our own toes are pinched.

Experience has already taught us in this war that hold-ing these smoky localities responsible for the confla-grations within them has a very salutary effect.

ON SLAVERY

AS A CONSTITUTIONAL QUESTION

I have no purpose, directly or indirectly, to interfere with the institution of slavery in the States where it ex-ists. I believe I have no lawful right to do so, and I have no inclination to do so.

Equal justice to the South, it is said, requires us to con-sent to the extension of slavery to new countries [states]. That is to say, inasmuch as you do not object to my tak-ing my hog to Nebraska, therefore I must not object to your taking your slave. Now, I admit this is perfectly logical, if there is no difference between hogs and Ne-groes.

. . . the thing is hid away, in the Constitution just as an afflicted man hides away a wen or cancer, which he dares not cut out at once, lest he bleed to death; with the promise, nevertheless, that the cutting may begin at the end of a given time.

We must make good in essence as well as in form Madison's avowal that "the word *slave* ought not to appear in the Constitution"; and we must even go further and decree that only local law, and not that time-honored instrument [the Constitution] shall shelter a slaveholder.

I am naturally anti-slavery. If slavery is not wrong, nothing is wrong. . . . Yet I have never understood that the Presidency conferred upon me an unrestricted right to act officially on this judgment and feeling.

A QUESTION OF DEMOCRATIC PRINCIPLE

The monstrous injustice of slavery deprives our republican example of its just influence in the world—enables the enemies of free institutions, with plausibility, to taunt us as hypocrites.

As I would not be a slave, so I would not be a master. This expresses my idea of democracy. Whatever differs

from this, to the extent of the difference, is no democracy.

This is a world of compensation; and he who would be
no slave must consent to have no slave. Those who deny
freedom to others deserve it not for themselves, and,
under a just God, cannot long retain it.

I have always thought that all men should be free; but
if any should be slaves, it should be first those who desire it for themselves, and secondly those who desire it
for others. Whenever I hear anyone arguing for slavery,
I feel a strong impulse to see it tried on him personally.

The same spirit says, "You toil and work and earn bread,
and I'll eat it." No matter in what shape it comes,
whether from the mouth of a king who seeks to bestride
the people of his own nation and live by the fruit of
their labor, or from one race of men as an apology for enslaving another race, it is the same tyrannical principle.

In giving freedom to the slave, we assure freedom to the
free—honorable alike in what we give and what we preserve. We shall save or meanly lose the last, best hope of
earth.

Familiarize yourself with the chains of bondage and you prepare your own limbs to wear them. Accustomed to trample on the rights of others, you have lost the genius of your own independence and become the fit subject of the first cunning tyrant who rises among you.

If we cannot give freedom to every creature, let us do nothing that will impose slavery upon any other creature.

A NATIONAL CRISIS

"A house divided against itself cannot stand." I believe this government cannot endure, permanently half slave and half free. I do not expect the Union to be dissolved—I do not expect the house to fall—but I do expect it will cease to be divided.

AND A MORAL DILEMMA

Slavery is founded in the selfishness of man's nature—opposition to it, in his love of justice. These principles are an eternal agonism; and when brought into collision so fiercely, as slavery extension brings them, shocks and throes, and convulsions must ceaselessly follow.

I am not much of a judge of religion, but, in my opinion, the religion that sets men to rebel and fight against their government, because, as they think, that government does not sufficiently help some men to eat their bread in the sweat of other men's faces, is not the sort of religion upon which people get to heaven.

Both [slaveholder and slave] read the same Bible, and pray to the same God; and each invokes His aid against the other. It may seem strange that any men should dare to ask a just God's assistance in wringing their bread from the sweat of other men's faces.

I say that there is room enough for us all to be free, and that it does not wrong the white man that the Negro should be free, but it positively wrongs the mass of the white men that the Negro should be enslaved.

If the people should, by whatever mode or means, make it an executive duty to re-enslave such persons, another, and not I, must be their instrument to perform it.

If I could save the Union without freeing any slave, I would do it; and if I could save it by freeing all the slaves, I would do it; and, if I could save it by freeing some and leaving others alone, I would also do that.

My paramount object in this struggle is to save the Union, and is not either to save or to destroy slavery. . . . What I do about slavery and the colored race, I do because I believe it helps to save the Union.

American Slavery is one of those offenses which, in the providence of God . . . He now wills to remove [through] this terrible war, as the woe due to those by whom the offense came. . . . Fondly do we hope—fervently do we pray—that this mighty scourge of war may speedily pass away. Yet if God wills that it continue, until all the wealth piled by the bondman's two hundred and fifty years of unrequited toil shall be sunk, and until every drop of blood drawn with the lash, shall be paid by another drawn with the sword, as was said three thousand years ago, so still it must be said "the judgments of the Lord, are true and righteous altogether."

On a Society of Equals

I have said that in their right to "life, liberty and the pursuit of happiness," as proclaimed in that old Declaration, the inferior races are our equals.

Fourscore and seven years ago our fathers brought forth on this continent, a new nation, conceived in Liberty, and dedicated to the proposition that all men are created equal . . .

Advancement—improvement in condition—is the order of things in a society of equals.

No oppressed people will fight and endure as our fathers did without the promise of something better than a mere change of masters.

You cannot institute any equality between right and wrong.

Equality in society alike beats inequality, whether the latter be of the British aristocratic sort or the domestic slavery sort.

When we were the political slaves of King George, and wanted to be free, we called the maxim that "all men are created equal" a self-evident truth, but now when we have grown fat, and have lost all dread of being slaves ourselves, we have become so greedy to be masters that we call the same maxim a "self-evident lie." The Fourth of July has not quite dwindled away; it is still a great day—for burning firecrackers!!!

Our progress in degeneracy appears to me to be pretty rapid. As a nation we began by declaring that "all men are created equal." We now practically read it "all men are created equal except Negroes." When the Know-Nothings get control, it will read "all men are created equal except Negroes and foreigners and Catholics." When it comes to this, I shall prefer emigrating to some country where they make no pretense of loving liberty—to Russia, for instance, where despotism can be taken pure, and without the base alloy of hypocrisy.

There is no reason in the world why the Negro is not entitled to all the natural rights enumerated in the Declaration of Independence, the right to life, liberty and the pursuit of happiness. I hold that he is as much entitled to these as the white man. I agree with Judge [Senator] Douglas he is not equal in many respects— certainly not in color, perhaps not in moral or intellectual endowment. But in the right to eat the bread, without leave of anybody else, which his own hand earns, *he is my equal and the equal of Judge Douglas, and the equal of every living man.*

Every man, black, white or yellow, has a mouth to be fed and two hands with which to feed it—and that bread should be allowed to go to that mouth without controversy.

All I ask for the Negro is that if you do not like him, let him alone. If God gave him but little, that little let him enjoy.

If it was like two wrecked seamen on a narrow plank; where each must push the other off or drown himself, I would push the Negro off or the white man either, but it is not; the plank is large enough for both.

I protest against the counterfeit logic which concludes that, because I do not want a black woman for a slave, I must necessarily want her for a wife. I need not have her for either. I can just leave her alone.

There is an unwillingness on the part of our people for you free colored people to remain with us. Whether it is right or wrong I do not propose to discuss, but to propose it as a fact with which we have to deal. It is better for us both, therefore, to be separated.

Shall we free them and make them politically and socially our equals? My own feelings will not admit of this, and if they would the feelings of the great mass of white people would not. Whether this accords with strict justice or not is not the sole question. A universal feeling, whether well or ill-founded, cannot safely be disregarded. We cannot then make them our equals.

Negro equality! Fudge!! How long, in the government of a God great enough to make and maintain this Universe, shall there continue knaves to vend, and fools to gulp, so low a piece of demagoguery as this.

I have never seen to my knowledge a man, woman or child who was in favor of producing a perfect equality, social and political, between Negroes and white men.

I am not, nor ever have been in favor of bringing about in any way the social and political equality of the white and black races. I am not, nor ever have been in favor of making voters or jurors of Negroes, nor of qualifying them to hold office, nor to intermarry with white people; and I will say in addition to this that there is a physical difference between the white and black races which I believe will for ever forbid the two races living together on terms of social and political equality. And inasmuch as they cannot so live, while they do remain together there must be the position of superior and inferior, and I as much as any other man am in favor of having the superior assigned to the white race.

Anything that argues me into his idea of perfect social and political equality with the Negro is but a specious and fantastic arrangement of words, by which a man can prove a horse-chestnut to be a chestnut horse.

Let us discard all this quibbling about this man and the other man—this race and that race and the other race being inferior, and therefore they must be placed in an inferior position . . .

I . . . should, as the principle, treat them [freed blacks] precisely as I would treat the same number of free white people in the same relation and condition.

[On Black Voters]
They would probably help, in some trying time to come, to keep the jewel of liberty within the family of freedom.

What I would most desire would be the separation of the white and black races.

ON SPEECHMAKING

Reading from speeches is a tedious business, particularly for an old man that has to put on spectacles, and the more so if the man be so tall that he has to bend over to the light.

Henry Clay's eloquence did not consist, as many fine specimens of eloquence do, of types and figures, of antitheses and elegant arrangements of words and sentences, but rather of that deeply earnest and impassioned tone and manner which can proceed only through conviction in the speaker of the justice and importance of his cause. This it is that truly touches the chords of sympathy; and those who heard Mr. Clay never failed to be moved by it, or ever after forgot the impression. All his efforts were made for practical effect. He never spoke merely to be heard.

I mean to put a case no stronger than the truth will allow.

If a man says he knows a thing, then he must show how he knows it.

There are two ways of establishing a proposition. One is by trying to demonstrate it upon reason, and the other is to show that great men in former times have thought so and so, and thus to pass it by the weight of pure authority.

If a man will stand up and assert, and repeat and re-assert, that two and two do not make four, I know nothing in the power of argument that can stop him. I think I can answer the Judge so long as he sticks to the premises; but when he flies from them, I cannot work any argument into the consistency of a mental gag and actually close his mouth with it.

This is as plain as adding up the weight of three small hogs.

The speech at New York . . . went off passably well and gave me no trouble whatever. The difficulty was to make nine others, before reading audiences who had already seen all my ideas in print.

I wish to avoid both the substance and the appearance of dictation.

As to speech making, by way of getting the hang of the House I made a little speech two or three days ago on a post-office question of no general interest. I find speaking here and elsewhere about the same thing. I was about as badly scared, and no worse, as I am when I speak in court.

And now, my friends, have I said enough? There appears to be a difference of opinion between you and me, and I feel called upon to insist upon deciding the question myself.

You speak of Lincoln stories. I don't think that's the correct phrase. I don't make the stories mine by telling them.

It's not the story itself, but its purpose, or effect that interests me.

[Responding to criticism of his storytelling]
I have found in the course of a long experience that common people—common people, take them as they run, are more easily influenced and informed through the medium of a broad illustration than in any other way, and as to what the hypercritical few may think, I don't care.

I remember how, when a mere child, I used to get irritated when anybody talked to me in a way I could not understand. . . . I can remember going to my little bedroom, after hearing the neighbors talk of an evening with my father, and spending the night walking up and down, and trying to make out what was the exact meaning of some of their, to me, dark sayings. I could not sleep . . . when I got on such a hunt after an idea, until I had caught it; and when I thought I had got it, I was not satisfied . . . until I had put it in language plain enough, as I thought, for any boy I knew to comprehend. This was a passion with me, and it has stuck by me.

He can compress the most words into the smallest ideas better than any man I ever met.

So hard is it to have a thing understood as it really is.

In my present position it is hardly proper for me to make speeches. Every word is so closely noted that it will not do to make foolish ones, and I cannot be expected to be prepared to make sensible ones. If I were as I have been for most of my life, I might, perhaps, talk nonsense to you for half an hour, and it wouldn't hurt anybody.

The world will little note nor long remember what we say here.

I am very little inclined on any occasion to say anything unless I hope to produce some good by it.

I have made a great many speeches in my life, and I feel considerably relieved now to know that the dignity of the position in which I have been placed does not permit me to expose myself any longer.

On Temperance

The practice of drinking . . . is just as old as the world itself. . . . It commonly entered into the first draught of the infant and the last draught of the dying man.

Many were greatly injured by it; but none seemed to think the injury arose from the use of a bad thing, but from the abuse of a very good thing.

Prohibition will work great injury to the cause of Temperance. It is a species of intemperance within itself, for it attempts to control a man's appetite by legislation and makes a crime out of things that are not crimes. A prohibition law strikes at the very principles upon which our government was founded.

Whether or not the world would be vastly benefited by a total and final banishment from it of all intoxicating drinks seems to me now to be an open question. Three-fourths of mankind confess the affirmative with their tongues, and, I believe, all the rest acknowledge it in their hearts.

I remember being once amused at seeing two particularly intoxicated men engaged in a fight with their great coats on, which fight, after a long and rather harmless contest, ended in each having fought himself out of his own coat and into that of the other.

If the relative grandeur of revolutions shall be estimated by the great amount of human misery they alleviate, and the small amount they inflict, then, indeed, this [temperance] will be the grandest the world shall ever have seen.

In my judgment, such of us as have never fallen victims, have been spared more from the absence of appetite, than from any mental or moral superiority over those who have.

When the victory shall be complete—when there shall be neither a slave nor a drunkard on the earth.

WORDS ON & TO THE
UNION ARMY

Beware of rashness, but with energy and sleepless vigilance go forward and give us victories.

Hold on with a bull-dog grip, and chew and choke as much as possible.

Only those generals who gain successes can set up dictators. What I now ask of you is military success, and I will risk the dictatorship.

All you have to do is keep the faith, to remain steadfast to the right, to stand by your banner. Nothing should lead you to leave your guns. Stand together, ready, with match in hand. Allow nothing to turn you to the right or to the left. . . . Victory, complete and permanent, is sure at the last.

Passion has helped us; but can do so no more. It will in future be our enemy. Reason, cold, calculating, unimpassioned reason, must furnish all the materials for our future support and defense.

I do believe our army chaplains, taken as a class, are the worst men we have in our service.

Gold is good in its place, but living, brave, patriotic men are better than gold.

[Mocking Cowardice]
Captain, I have as brave a heart as Julius Caesar ever had; but, somehow or other, whenever danger approaches, my cowardly legs will run away with it.

ON ARMY PAYMASTERS

Please say to these gentlemen that if they do not work quickly I will make quick work with them.

[Approached by a paymaster at a public reception]
"Being here, Mr. Lincoln, I thought I'd call and pay my respects."

"From the complaints of the soldiers," responded Lincoln, "I guess that's about all any of you do pay."

[When asked how many men the Confederate Army had in the field]

Twelve hundred thousand, according to the best authority. . . . You see, all of our Generals, when they get whipped, say the enemy outnumbers them from three or five to one, and I must believe them. We have four hundred thousand men in the field, and three times four make twelve. Don't you see it?

It is called the Army of the Potomac, but is only McClellan's bodyguard.

[Exasperated with General George B. McClellan for underestimating his own strength, and overestimating that of the enemy]

Sending troops to [McClellan] is like shoveling flies across the barnyard—most of them never seem to get there.

McClellan has the slows.

McClellan is doing nothing to make himself respected or feared.

My dear McClellan,
If you don't want to use the army, I should like to borrow it for a while.

Yours respectfully,
Abraham Lincoln

[On General Joe Hooker who, rushing headlong into action, sent his dispatches from "Headquarters in the Saddle"]
The trouble with Hooker is that he's got his headquarters where his hindquarters ought to be.

I believed that General Meade and his noble army had expended all the skill, and toil, and blood, up to the ripe harvest, and then let the crop go to waste.

[On complaints that Ulysses S. Grant was a drunk]
I can't spare this man—he fights.

Let me know what brand of whiskey Grant uses. For if it makes fighting generals like Grant, I should like to get some of it for distribution.

[To a busybody who complained that Grant drank twelve bottles at one sitting]
That's more than I can swallow.

[Describing the tactic whereby Grant held Lee's army under siege at Petersburg, while Sherman marched through South Carolina and Georgia]

Grant has the bear by the leg while Sherman takes off the hide.

The most interesting news we now have is from Sherman. We all know where he went in, but I can't tell where he will come out.

ON THE ENEMY

[Jefferson] Davis is right. His army is his only hope, not only against us, but against his own people. If that were crushed the people would be ready to swing back to their old bearings.

We are contending with the enemy, who, as I understand, drives every able-bodied man he can reach into his ranks, very much as a butcher drives bullocks into a slaughter pen.

ON THE ENLISTMENT OF BLACKS

The bare sight of fifty thousand armed, and drilled black soldiers on the banks of the Mississippi, would end the rebellion at once. And who doubts that we can prevent that sight, if we but take hold in earnest?

. . . the emancipation policy, and the use of colored troops, constitute the heaviest blow yet dealt to the rebellion.

On What's Right

Stand with anybody that stands for RIGHT. Stand with him while he is right and PART with him when he goes wrong.

The probability that we may fail in the struggle ought not to deter us from the support of a cause we believe to be just.

. . . right and wrong . . . They are the two principles that have stood face to face from the beginning of time; and will ever continue to struggle. The one is the common right of humanity, and the other the divine right of kings. It is the same principle in whatever shape it develops itself. . . . No matter in what shape it comes, whether from the mouth of a king who seeks to bestride the people of his own nation and live by the fruit of their labor, or from one race of men as an apology for enslaving another race, it is the same tyrannical principle.

I know that the Lord is always on the side of the right, but it is my constant anxiety and prayer that I and this nation should be on the Lord's side.

[A plea for voluntary emancipation by border states]
That makes an issue; and the burden of proof is upon. I do not argue. I beseech you to make the arguments for yourselves. You can not, if you would, be blind to the signs of the times.

Groping for some middle ground between the right and the wrong, vain as the search for a man who should be neither a living man nor a dead man . . .

[Addressing the Temperance Society of Springfield, Illinois]
There is something so ludicrous in promises of good, or threats of evil, a great way off, as to render the whole subject with which they are connected, easily turned into ridicule. "Better lay down that spade your stealing, Paddy,— if you don't you'll pay for it at the day of judgment." "By the powers, if ye'll credit me so long, I'll take another."

The true rule, in determining to embrace or reject any-thing is not whether it have any evil in it, but whether it have more of evil than of good. There are few things wholly evil or wholly good.

ON WOMEN

A woman is the only thing that I am afraid of that I know will not hurt me.

Others have been made fools of by the girls, but this can never with truth be said of me. I most emphatically, in this instance, made a fool of myself.

[After rejection by Mary Owen]
I have now come to the conclusion never again to think of marrying, and for this reason: I can never be satisfied with anyone who would be blockhead enough to have me.

The very first invention was a joint operation, Eve hav-ing shared with Adam the getting up of the apron. And, indeed, judging from the fact that sewing has come down to our times as "woman's work" it is very probable she took the leading part—he, perhaps, doing no more than to stand by and thread the needle.

I am not accustomed to the use of language of eulogy; I have never studied the art of paying compliments to women; but I must say, that if all that has been said by orators and poets since the creation of the world in praise of women were applied to the women of America, it would not do them justice for their conduct during this war. I close by saying, God bless the women of America.

Please have the Adjutant General ascertain whether 2nd. Lieut. of Co. D. 2nd. Infantry—Alexander E. Drake, is not entitled to promotion. His wife thinks he is.

Whatever woman may cast her lot with mine, should any ever do so, it is my intention to do all in my power to make her happy and contented; and there is nothing I can imagine that would make me more unhappy than to fail in the effort.

I want in all cases to do right, and most particularly so in all cases with women.

I know not how much is within the legal power of the government in this case; but it is certainly true in equity, that the laboring women in our employment should be paid at the least as much as they were at the beginning of the war. Will the Secretary of War please have the cases fully examined, and so much relief given as can be consistently with the law and the public service.

On Virtues & Vices

It has been my experience that folks who have no vices have very few virtues.

ON CHARACTER

Character is like a tree and reputation like its shadow. The shadow is what we think of it; the tree is the real thing.

ON PATIENCE

The best thing about the future is that it only comes one day at a time.

Things may come to those who wait, but only the things left by those who hustle.

It's better to be silent and thought a fool than speak and remove all doubt.

ON COVETOUSNESS

The way for a young man to rise is to improve himself every way he can, never suspecting that anybody wishes to hinder him. Allow me to assure you that suspicion and jealousy never did help any man in any situation. There may sometimes be ungenerous attempts to keep a young man down; and they will succeed, too, if he allows his mind to be diverted from its true channel to brood over the attempted injury.

ON INTOLERANCE

Intensity of thought . . . will sometimes wear the sweetest idea threadbare and turn it to the bitterness of death.

On Liberty

My faith in the proposition that each man should do precisely as he pleases with all which is exclusively his own, lies at the foundation of the sense of justice there is in me.

The legitimate object of government is to do for a community of people whatever they need to have done, but cannot do at all, or cannot so well do, for themselves, in their separate and individual capacities. In all that the people can individually do as well for themselves, government ought not to interfere.

You cannot keep out of trouble by spending more than you earn. You cannot bring about prosperity by discouraging thrift. You cannot strengthen the weak by weakening the strong. You cannot lift the wage earner by pulling down the wage payer. You cannot help the poor by destroying the rich. You cannot build character and courage by taking away a man's initiative and independence. You cannot help men permanently by doing for them what they could and should do for themselves.

It is the duty of nations as well as of men to own their dependence upon the overruling power of God.

AND LIBERTY TO . . .

The world has never had a good definition of the word liberty. . . . The shepherd drives the wolf from the sheep's throat, for which the sheep thanks the shepherd as his liberator, while the wolf denounces him for the same act, as the destroyer of liberty, especially as the sheep was a black one. Plainly, the sheep and the wolf are not agreed upon a definition of liberty.

What constitutes the bulwark of our own liberty and independence? It is not our frowning battlements, our bristling sea coasts, our army and our navy. These are not our reliance against tyranny. . . . Our reliance is in the love of liberty which God has planted in us. Our defense is in the spirit which prized liberty as the heritage of all men, in all lands everywhere. Destroy this spirit and you have planted the seeds of despotism at your own doors.

[On the Declaration of Independence]
the electric cord . . . that links the hearts of patriotic and liberty-loving men together . . .

Many free countries have lost their liberty, and ours may lose hers; but if she shall, be it my proudest plume, not that I was the last to desert, but that I never deserted her.

On Agriculture & the American Landscape

Every blade of grass is a study; and to produce two where there was but one is both a profit and a pleasure.

Population must increase rapidly, more rapidly than in former times, and ere long the most valuable of all the arts will be the art of deriving a comfortable subsistence from the smallest area of soil.

[On Niagara Falls]
It calls upon the indefinite past. . . . The Mammoth and Mastodon—now so long dead, that fragments of their monstrous bones alone testify that they ever lived, have gazed on Niagara. In that long, long time, never still for a single moment. Never dried, never froze, never slept, never rested . . .

[Asked what had made the deepest impression on him when he saw Niagara Falls]
The thing that struck me most forcibly was, where in the world did all that water come from?

[On the Mississippi River and the end of the Civil War]
The Father of the Waters again goes unvexed to the sea.

[Lincoln, traveling on a train somewhere near Kansas, asks a fellow passenger the name of a small stream]
"It's called The Weeping Water"
"You remember," said Lincoln, "the laughing water up in Minnesota, called Minnehaha. Now, I think, this should be Minneboohoo."

ABRAHAM LINCOLN

Abraham Lincoln was born 12 February 1809 some-where backwoods of Hardin, Kentucky. He spent his early years in Kentucky and Indiana, but came of age in Illinois. Lincoln capitalized on his frontier days in later years, but as a young man he wanted nothing but to escape from it. While he was an able and hard worker, Lincoln inherited none of his father's westering spirit and opted instead for a townsman's career in law and politics.

He moved to New Salem, Illinois, where he worked for others and studied law on his own. In 1833, he was appointed Postmaster. One year later, Lincoln entered the state legislature as a Whig member. After two more years, he was admitted to the bar. He would stay with the state legislature until 1842, when he decided to settle down and concentrate on his law practice. He married Mary Todd, the daughter of a prominent Springfield Family. Four years later, a seat of Congress captured his attention. Lincoln was elected in 1846 and served a single term. He returned home after two years a bit disillusioned with national politics, and eager to return to his law practice in Springfield.

Lincoln returned to national politics during the turmoil of the 1850s. He spoke out against the Kansas-Nebraska Act (1854) and the *Dred Scott* decision (1857). The former had repealed the Missouri Compromise of 1820 and paved the way for slavery's entry to the territories while the latter, a Supreme Court decision, posited that the "due process" clause of the Fifth Amendment ensured a slaveowner's right to take his human property into the territories and have it protected there. Although Lincoln opposed the expansion of slavery into the territories, he was not an abolitionist. Lincoln acceded that the practice of slavery in the South was protected under the Constitution. He was thus also a staunch supporter of fugitive slave laws.

In 1856, Lincoln joined the Republican Party. Two years later, the Republican Party voted on a platform to contain slavery and nominated Lincoln as their candidate for senator from Illinois. Lincoln accepted that nomination with his "A House Divided" speech, and challenged the Democratic incumbent Stephen A. Douglas to a series of public debates. The contest between these two men captured the public imagination and, while Douglas was reelected, Lincoln won national recognition for his plainspoken eloquence, a style of public speaking that clearly parted from the more florid rhetoric of the age. One moment of those debates, in particular, assured Lincoln increasing visibility. During the debate at Freeport, Illinois, Lincoln stumped Douglas asking him what, considering the recent *Dred Scott* decision, recourse did the inhabitants of a territory have to legislate either for or against slavery before statehood? In 1860, Lincoln was named the Republican Party's candidate for the presidency.

His old rival, Stephen A. Douglas was also nominated for the presidency in 1860, but a rift in Democratic Party politics resulted in his sharing the platform with John C. Breckenridge. Lincoln defeated both men, and John C. Bell of the Constitutional Union Party, winning only 40 percent of the popular vote but 180 electoral votes. Lincoln tried as president-elect to dispel rumors that he would be hostile to the South by restating his willingness to tolerate slavery where it already existed. But his opponents would not listen. And a full month before Lincoln took office, seven Southern states seceded from the Union to form the Confederate States of America.

On 12 April 1861, Lincoln sent a military expedition to resupply Fort Sumter in Charleston Harbor and, in retaliation, the Confederates attacked the fort. When Lincoln called for 75,000 to quash the rebellion, four more states seceded and the conflict escalated to civil war.

As a war president, Lincoln exercised the full extent of his powers as chief executive and commander in chief of the armed forces. Some would say he even overstepped his authority. Lincoln expanded the army without congressional authorization, he declared martial law, and suspended the writ of habeas corpus. Lincoln's largest step, or infraction as others saw it, was the Emancipation Proclamation. Effective 1 January 1863, Lincoln declared free all slaves in the area of rebellion. He did so as a "fit and necessary war measure," which might transform the 3 million slaves in the Confederacy into an army of liberation. Because it was a military order, over 4 million slaves in the border states that remained in the Union, and another quarter million in Union-occupied Tennessee and other areas under control of Federal armies were excluded from the language of the Proclamation. To have included them would have gone against Lincoln's firm belief that he lacked the constitutional means to abolish slavery in a time of peace.

Lincoln's stand on the issue of slavery is perhaps the best example of his pragmatic, yet principled politics. He personally abhorred slavery, but was not a reformer by political nature. He knew that if the War between the States were converted into a crusade against slavery, it would alienate a large part of the Union. The North would go to war to save the Union, but not to fight for blacks. Lincoln also knew that slavery was more than a moral issue; it was a matter of custom, law, and economy and its upset would fall nothing short of revolutionary. Lincoln was no optimist when it came to the nation's racial problem and, lacking a solution, he favored segregation as the best hope for peace.

Lincoln won reelection in 1864 by the skin of his teeth. In April 1865 the Union victory was secure and he began planning a policy of reconstruction. He oversaw passage of the Thirteenth Amendment that legally ended slavery. Intent on restoring the Union "with malice toward none," he authored a plan for the South's reentry into the Union based on the president's power to pardon. But one Confederate sympathizer would not forgive Lincoln. John Wilkes Booth assassinated Lincoln while attending a play at Ford's Theater in Washington, D.C., on 14 April 1865.